50 Life and Business Lessons from Elon Musk

Written by: George Ilian

Cover Illustration: Iren Flowers

Copyright © 2015

All Rights Reserved

All rights reserved. No part of this book may be reproduced or transmitted in any form or by any means, electronic or mechanical, including photocopying, recording or by any information storage and retrieval system, without written permission from the publisher, except for the inclusion of brief quotations in a review.

Warning-Disclaimer

The purpose of this book is to educate and entertain. The author or publisher does not guarantee that anyone following the techniques, suggestions, tips, ideas, or strategies will become successful. The author and publisher shall have neither liability or responsibility to anyone with respect to any loss or damage caused or alleged to be caused, directly or indirectly by the information contained in this book.

More Books By George Ilian

George Ilian is the author of many inspirational books and guides how to make money online.

His mission is to help you have all the money and freedom you need to go and live anywhere you want and travel around the world. It is all possible with the money that you can make online, giving you the ability to have everything you've ever wanted—and more!

Introduction

Whatever skeptics have said can't be done, Elon has gone out and made real. Remember in the 1990s, when we would call strangers and give them our credit-card numbers? Elon dreamed up a little thing called PayPal. His Tesla Motors and SolarCity companies are making a clean, renewable-energy future a reality...his SpaceX [is] reopening space for exploration...it's a paradox that Elon is working to improve our planet at the same time he's building spacecraft to help us leave it.

Richard Branson

It wouldn't be too much of a stretch to describe Elon Musk - one of the most imaginative entrepreneurs of the 21st century - as a living legend. Richard Branson has espoused his virtues, he has been favourably compared to visionary American industrialists such Henry Ford and John D. Rockefeller, and when Jon Favreau, the producer of *Iron Man*, was making the film, he even sent Robert Downey, Jr. to spend time with Musk in the SpaceX factory so that he could get some inspiration for his character.

But for Musk, at least, it is not all about him. The estimated $12.9 billion he has made in business are almost a side show: he is bored of journalists taking an interest in him, and wants to talk far more about his work, his companies, and what they are doing to change the world. In order to get under the skin of his success (and, one hopes, to be able to replicate it), you need to be able to understand two things: WHY Musk is doing what he is doing; and HOW he is able to do these things. He thinks, and does, things differently to everyone else, and that's why studying his lessons is invaluable.

This book - part biography, part self-help tool - is intended to inform you about the life, ideas, approach and work of Elon Musk to date. There is, after all, likely to be much more to come from this extraordinarily innovative entrepreneur. We have endeavoured to analyse his actions, strengths and weaknesses, and to summarise them into 50 short, memorable lessons that you can action in your own personal and commercial life. We can't guarantee that you will be as successful as Musk, but you will gain a level of insight. The book is designed to be easily digestible by a layman reader, but also to have sufficient detail that those with a specific interest in one or more of Musk's business, or in his unique style of leadership, will also be able to take away something of value.

The first section of this book examines Musk's family background and education. This is to help you understand where the man is coming from, what it is that makes him the man he is. There are certainly a few indications of his early precocity and, indeed, virtuosity, and you will recognise the names of several key characters who have remained with him into adulthood, contributing notably to his success.

Lesson 1: Success is not about an individual. It is also about the team that has got them into the position where they can succeed.

We then look at Musk's business endeavours in turn, starting with Zip2 and x.com (later PayPal), the two internet start-ups that catapulted Musk from being an ordinary geek in Silicon Valley to being a multi millionaire who everyone else wanted to work with. There is substantial coverage of SpaceX and Tesla Motors, probably the two most exciting and groundbreaking of Musk's enterprises, but also of SolarCity and the Hyperloop, an idea that seems to have had its origins in the science fiction obsession of Musk's early childhood.

In the final section of the book we examine the rewards and accolades that Musk has received, his politics and beliefs, and his private life. Although the public persona is one of great confidence and success, Musk has known pain and tragedy too. His personal relationships have been scrutinised by the press, and have at a times fallen victim to his complete addiction to his work, to his wealth, and to his ego. Musk has his challenges in that regard, and so here the lessons you can learn might well be about what not to do, rather than simply emulating his behaviour.

Background and Education

Born on 28 June, 1971, Elon Musk is one of the youngest, and most dynamic, of the world's self-made billionaires. He is of mixed ancestry - his father, though born in South Africa, is of British and Pennsylvania Dutch origin, and his mother is a Canadian - and he was born in Pretoria, South Africa, the eldest of three children. His siblings are his brother, fellow entrepreneur Kimbal Musk, and a sister, Tosca Musk. Their parents, Errol and Maye Musk, divorced in 1980, after which Musk lived mostly with his father.

In South Africa Musk was privately educated, first at Waterkloof House Preparatory School in Pretoria, where fellow alumni include the professional golfer Richard Stearne and international cricketer Eddie Barlow. The young Musk was bullied throughout his childhood, including on one particularly serious occasion when he was thrown down a flight of stairs and beaten unconscious. He was an academic child, always buried in a book, sometimes for up to 10 hours a day according to his brother. He was addicted to science fiction but also heavy-weight non-fiction books such as the *Encyclopaedia Britannica*.

He goes into his brain, and then you just see he is in another world. He still does that. Now I just leave him be because I know he is designing a new rocket or something.

Maye Musk

As far as Musk was concerned, education was simply "downloading data and algorithms into your brain," and hence he found conventional classroom learning exceptionally slow and frustrating. Almost everything he did learn was from his own reading, not from the classroom.

Lesson 2: A conventional education isn't for everyone. Sometimes the most important lessons are those we can teach ourselves.

Musk got his first computer when he was nine years old. The *How to Program guide* was supposed to take the user six months to complete, but Musk mastered it in three days. He developed a basic video game, Blastar, using BASIC. He describes it as "a trivial game…but better than Flappy Bird." The precocious teen sold this game to *PC and Office Technology* magazine for $500, equivalent to around $1,200 today. You can still find the game online and play it.

Lesson 3: You are never too young to start being an entrepreneur. Have faith in your ideas, and encourage your children to develop theirs too.

Leaving school, Musk decided not to stay in South Africa: he didn't relate well to the culture and felt that his entrepreneurial skills would be far better deployed across the pond. And so he emigrated to Canada, where his mother's nationality gave him citizenship rights. He enrolled at Queen's University in summer 1989 (where he would meet his first wife, Justine), and after four years (the second half of which was spent at the University of Pennsylvania), Musk graduated with a BSc in physics and a BA in economics. Showing his entrepreneurial streak early, Musk and fellow student Adeo Ressi (who went on to become the founder and CEO of TheFunded and The Founder Institute, as well as a board member of the X Prize Foundation) purchased a 10-bedroom frat house at the university and ran it as a nightclub.

Lesson 4: The relationships - personal and professional - that you establish in college might well be some of the most important you ever have. Maintain your friendships and associations, and support one another.

If you go back a few hundred years, what we take for granted today would seem like magic – being able to talk to people over long distances, to transmit images, flying, accessing vast amounts of data like an oracle. These are all things that would have been considered magic a few hundred years ago.

Elon Musk

From Pennsylvania, Musk moved across the US to California to take up a PhD offer at Stanford University. The lure of neighbouring Silicon Valley proved irresistible to the 24-year old Musk, however, and he lasted just two days on the course. Even as a student, there was a pressing question on his mind: What will most affect the future of humanity? The five answers that he came up with, the internet; sustainable energy; space exploration, in particular the permanent extension of life beyond Earth; artificial intelligence; and reprogramming the human genetic code, would determine his future direction as an entrepreneur.

Lesson 5: *As an entrepreneur you have to know what is important to you. Once you have established this, it will dictate the direction you and your businesses follow.*

Getting Started

Fresh out of college, Musk knew he had to get onto the Internet bandwagon or forever be left behind. He marched into the lobby of Netscape, uninvited, but was too nervous to talk to anyone or ask for a job, so he turned tail and walked out again. Starting his own business seemed less nerve-wracking, and Musk decided to keep it in the family. He joined forces with his younger brother Kimbal (also a successful entrepreneur, and now with business interests in technology, health and food sectors) to create a software company called Zip2. The first $28,000 of start-up capital came from their father, Errol Musk.

Lesson 6: Take advantage of the capital - human and financial - that is available to you. Be grateful for it and deploy it in such away that everyone who contributes will benefit.

Zip2 has been described as, "a primitive combination of Yelp and Google Maps, far before anything like either of those existed". The Musks worked around the clock, sleeping in the office and showering at the local YMCA.

Work like hell. I mean you just have to put in 80 to 100 hour weeks every week. [This] improves the odds of success. If other people are putting in 40 hour workweeks and you're putting in 100 hour workweeks, then even if you're doing the same thing, you know that you will achieve in four months what it takes them a year to achieve.

Elon Musk

Zip2 developed, hosted and maintained consumer websites for media companies and enabled those companies to target their services at specific groups of online customers. Many companies couldn't see the appeal of the Internet - what was wrong with a listing in the Yellow Pages? - but as recognition of the potential of the internet increased, so too did the appeal of Zip2's offering. Simply but professionally designed, the software was bought by more than 200 media clients including the *New York Times* and the *Chicago Tribune*. Musk was client facing and a strong salesman, gaining the company new contacts and business relationships, but his own board had concerns about his management technique and they blocked his bids to become CEO.

Lesson 7: However great your idea, there is no substitute for hard graft and the right timing. All three of these

things need to be in place if your business is going to be a success.

Compaq (now a division of HP) acquired Zip2 from the Musk brothers in 1999, just four years after they had founded the company. Compaq paid $307 million in cash, plus a further $34 million in stock options, and so overnight both Elon and Kimbal became multi millionaires. Elon alone is thought to have made $22 million from the deal.

Financial Services

Musk took $10 million of his earnings from Zip2 and reinvested it straight away into a venture called x.com. This was an online banking and email payments company, and Musk was confident that the internet banking and money transfer was a business about to explode. He was right.

Lesson 8: If you have a gut hunch about the potential of an emerging market, be prepared to put your money where your mouth is. Only then can you test the waters and benefit from the upswing.

X.com wasn't the only start-up operating in this field, however: Confinity, trading as PayPal, had also recently been launched as a payment platform for handheld devices. The two companies were operating out of the same building, and recognising that there was no point in going head to head if they could work together and dominate the market, they merged in 2000.

Lesson 9: You won't always be the only person to have come up with a great idea. Sometimes you'll have to weigh up the pros and cons of competition v joining forces.

The merger didn't go especially smoothly. There were a lot of big egos in the room, all of them successful internet entrepreneurs in their own rights. Whilst Musk was on a fund-raising trip / honeymoon with his first wife, his partners staged a coup and replaced Musk as CEO with Peter Thiel. Musk disagreed with the decision, but had to accept it. At the same time, Musk wanted the joint company to continue trading as x.com, thinking that the names Confinity and PayPal would quickly date. Customer surveys showed, however, that the general public equated the name x.com with something that was x-rated, which was a serious stumbling block for the brand. Musk was therefore forced to admit defeat and reverted to using the name PayPal in 2001.

In hindsight, this was the right decision: PayPal was clear about what it did in a way that x.com was not. The company focused exclusively on online payments, with x.com terminating its other banking services.

Lesson 10: We are all learning throughout our careers. Everyone needs to be humble and to be able to bounce back when they have made a mistake.

PayPal grew rapidly on the back of a viral marketing campaign: new subscribers were automatically recruited when they received funds using the software. It was simple to use, free for buyers, affordable for sellers, and answered growing needs for better financial security online. The company went public in October 2002 and Musk alone (who was PayPal's largest shareholder) netted $165 million in eBay stock. The total value of PayPal at the time of the acquisition was $1.5 billion. Musk had been catapulted into the big time.

Space: The Final Frontier?

Going from PayPal, I thought: 'Well, what are some of the other problems that are likely to most affect the future of humanity?' Not from the perspective, 'What's the best way to make money?'

Elon Musk

Before the ink was even dry on the sale of PayPal to eBay, Musk was already looking at his options for the future. He had always been fascinated by space and space technology, and he wanted to both reinvigorate our interest in space exploration and get increased funding for NASA, both of which had largely fallen by the wayside since the end of the Cold War. His first idea was to create a Mars Oasis, a miniature greenhouse project on the red planet where he could experiment with growing food crops.

Lesson 11: Sometimes even the sky isn't the limit. If you have a dream, however hard it might be to realise it, that doesn't mean you shouldn't try to make it happen. Giant leaps forward demand giant dreams!

Musk travelled to Russia with Jim Cantrell, a well-established fixer in the aerospace industry, and his old business partner Adeo Ressi. The three men planned to buy refurbished Dnepr-1 rockets, converted intercontinental ballistic missiles (ICBMs) that can be used to launch artificial satellites into space. They met with some major Russian aerospace companies, including NPO Lavochkin and Kosmotras, but the Russians didn't take them seriously: they had no experience in satellites or other areas of space technology, and look just to be wealthy time wasters. They returned home empty handed.

Lesson 12: Money alone doesn't buy you credibility. You need to do your research, plan, and bring in the right level of expertise if you want to be respected in new fields and markets.

They returned a year later, this time with Mike Griffin, formerly of NASA's Jet Propulsion Laboratory, who was at that time working with spacecraft and satellite manufacturer Orbital Sciences. On this occasion the group had more professional credibility, and Kosmotras therefore offered Musk one rocket for $8 million. Believing (probably quite rightly) that he was being screwed over, Musk stormed out of the meeting and headed for home. On the flight home he calculated that he could build his own rockets for the Mars Oasis far more cost effectively, estimating that the raw materials needed were only 3% of the total sales price of a rocket. Even enjoying a 70% gross margin, Musk reckoned he could cut the launch price by a factor of 10. Vertical integration and and a modular approach would be the keys. The seeds of SpaceX were sown.

Lesson 13: Applying models and strategies from different industries can make you huge savings in your own industry, particularly if you have the capacity and inclination to do things in house.

Musk's aim with SpaceX was to create a simple, inexpensive and reusable space rocket which would reduce the cost of space transportation and, ultimately, make viable the human colonisation of Mars.

Musk was determined to work with the best in the business from the word go, and so he approached Tom Mueller, an employee of aerospace conglomerate TRW Inc. and the inventor of the world's largest amateur liquid-fuel rocket engine, which was capable of producing 13,000 lbf (58 kN) of thrust. The two men founded SpaceX in El Segundo,

California, and they immediately got to work. Their first rocket, Falcon 1 (named in honour of *Star Wars*' Millennium Falcon) was developed and manufactured between 2006 and 2009 and became the first privately developed launch vehicle to go into orbit.

I think it is a mistake to hire huge numbers of people to get a complicated job done. Numbers will never compensate for talent in getting the right answer (two people who don't know something are no better than one), will tend to slow down progress, and will make the task incredibly expensive.

Elon Musk

Lesson 14: If you want to make the very best products, you have to hire the very best people in their field.

The Falcon 1 was a two-stage-to-orbit rocket completely designed by SpaceX. It had two engines, a Merlin engine and a Kestrel engine, and it was launched five times. On the last of these occasions it successfully delivered into orbit the Malaysian RazakSAT satellite. The rocket was then retired, making way for subsequent models (the Falcon 9, the Falcon Heavy and the Dragon) which utilised improved design features.

Lesson 15: Never rest on your laurels. You have to constantly be thinking of - and actioning - the next big idea if you want to keep ahead and ensure your offering is fresh.

Failure is an option here. If things are not failing, you are not innovating enough.

Elon Musk

The trajectory of SpaceX has not always been smooth: the first three test rockets all exploded before reaching orbit, leaving Musk with just enough money for one more try. It was fourth time lucky or that was it: no one was going to invest in the company until they had at least one successful launch. Luckily for Musk, the Falcon made it up into orbit on that fourth occasion.

Lesson 16: Make sure that you have sufficient cash reserves to carry you through your product development phase comfortably. You don't want to run out of money at the final hurdle and be left with nothing to show for your effort and expenditure.

In June 2015 a SpaceX rocket resupplying the International Space Station exploded just two minutes after launch. The likely cause was a failed steel strut holding down a canister of helium. In theory, the strut in question was designed to withstand 10,000 pounds of force, but it failed with just 20% of that force. This meant that the bottle shot to the top of the tank in the rocket's upper stage, causing helium to spew into the oxygen tank and over pressurise it. The rocket broke up into thousands of small parts and the Dragon cargo capsule it was carrying fell into the sea, along with its 4,000 pounds of supplies. Had the Dragon capsule been programmed with software to deploy its parachute, it may have survived, and so the next-generation version (which is expected eventually to carry crew members into orbit) will have that software as well as its own thrusters. SpaceX is sending its own, autonomous underwater vehicle to search for debris in a bid to better understand the cause of the accident and its impact on other parts of the craft. Remarkably, in spite of seven years of launches, this was the first such mishap SpaceX suffered. To give engineers time to learn lessons from the incident, the first Falcon Heavy launch will be pushed back until spring 2015, but it is not expected to have long-term detrimental impact on the company and its plans.

Lesson 17: One relatively small oversight or error can have dramatic consequences. Don't overlook the small things.

It is worth considering at this point the funding model for SpaceX. Although Musk did invest substantial amounts of his own fortune (an estimated $100 million by March 2006), he was by no means the only stakeholder. In 2008, $20 million in investment came from the Founders Fund (the venture capital fund behind PayPal, Spotify and Airbnb). The total budget of the company over the past 10 years has been in the region of $1 billion, of which the majority has come as income from development contracts. NASA alone has paid SpaceX somewhere in the region of $500 million. SpaceX has contracts for more than 40 space launches, and therefore gains revenue both from down payments and ongoing progress payments as each stage of a project is completed. Musk has retained approximately two-thirds of the company's shares, an eye watering sum given that after SpaceX's successful COTS 2+ flight in May 2012, the company was valued at $2.8 billion.

Lesson 18: Cash flow problems kill companies. You need to understand clearly exactly how much money will be needed at each stage of your business' growth, and where that money is going to come from.

Although there has been much discussion in the marketplace as to if and when SpaceX will have an IPO, Musk has personally stated that he plans to hold off on this until the Mars Colonial Transporter is flying regularly. In his own words, "I just don't want [SpaceX] to be controlled by some private equity firm that would milk it for near-term revenue". In practical terms, Musk has no need to make a public offering of shares: SpaceX is a cash cow, and there are plenty of private customers eager to lap up shares without having them publicly traded. In January 2015 Google and Fidelity (the venture capital arm of Fidelity Investments) spent $1 billion buying 8.333% of SpaceX, giving the entirety of SpaceX a valuation of $12 billion.

For Musk, SpaceX is not just about the money: he has plenty of that, and it is the challenge he has set himself that really excited him. We will talk more about his beliefs about life in outer space in *Politics and Beliefs*, but it warrants mention here that Musk believes it is feasible to put the first man on Mars by 2021. He made this claim in an interview with the *Wall Street Journal* in 2011. What is more, he doesn't expect this to be a one-off achievement: in June 2015 he went one stage further, telling etv.com that by 2035 thousands of rockets will be flying to Mars each year, enabling us to establish a self-sustaining space colony with more than one million inhabitants.

Lesson 19: You will put your best efforts into pursuing an idea if it excites you. Yes, there has to be a business case for the idea too, but it is far more rewarding (and more likely to succeed) if your business is also a passion.

SpaceX's low cost launch model has put significant pressure on its competitors to lower their prices, something which can only please Musk. An orbital launch from the Falcon Heavy costs just $1,000 per pound, spurring Arianespace (a European competitor) to request subsidies from the European Union to be able to compete. In 2014 SpaceX won nine out of 20 worldwide bids for commercial launch services, more than any other company. SpaceX has signed contracts with the United States Air Force, NASA and the United States Department of Defense in addition to its conventional commercial contracts.

Lesson 20: If you can provide a high-quality product or service at a competitive rate, customers will come to you and you will dominate your marketplace.

Transport and Energy

Tesla Motors takes its name and inspiration from the Serbian American physicist, electrical engineer and inventor, Nikola Tesla (1856-1943), who worked with Thomas Edison in New York and who in his own right made major contributions to the modern alternating current (AC) electricity supply system. Clearly a pin-up of Musk's (who himself has a BSc in physics, see *Background and Education*), the motor in the Tesla Roadstar is based almost entirely on Tesla's original 1882 design.

Lesson 21: The best ideas aren't necessarily new ideas. Be prepared to take products or services that already exist and rework and improve them for the modern world.

As with PayPal, Musk was not the founder of Tesla Motors: that credit falls to two men, engineer Martin Eberhard and his business partner Marc Tarpenning. Eberhard and Tarpenning founded Tesla Motors in summer 2003 with the principal aim of commercialising electric vehicles. They wanted to create first an aspirational sports car model which would show off the capabilities of the their technology, and then diversify into more mainstream, affordable models for ordinary families. Musk invested in Tesla Motors in February 2004 and joined the company as the Chairman of the board. He took an active interest in product development (though not in the day to day running of the business), and Eberhanrd credits Musk with the insistence on a carbon fibre reinforced polymer body, as well as the design of the power electronics module to the headlamps.

Lesson 22: If you find someone else who has a great idea, and you have the skills, connections and capital to make it happen, work together. You don't have to be the inventor!

Musk's investment in Tesla Motors was in the region of $7.5 million (which came from his personal funds), and this relatively modest investment made him the controlling investor in Tesla's first funding round. To any onlooker, Musk's investment was completely crazy, however much you like cars. The last successful automotive start-up in the US was Chrysler in 1925, and no one had ever made money out of electric cars. It looked like a bottomless pit for money, with little or no chance of a financial return. Surely

Musk wasn't just going to throw away everything he'd worked so hard to earn? Was he delusional?

When Henry Ford made cheap, reliable cars, people said, 'Nah, what's wrong with a horse?' That was a huge bet he made, and it worked.

Elon Musk

Lesson 23: If you want to make really big bucks, there will always be an element of risk involved. You need to do your homework and decide if the gamble is worth it, ignoring detractors if you think that the odds are indeed in your favour.

There's a tremendous bias against taking risks. Everyone is trying to optimize their ass-covering.

Elon Musk

And indeed the early years of Tesla Motors were far from smooth. Although the company (and Musk) were picking up awards for their designs, including the 2006 Global Green product design award and the 2007 Index Design award, both for the Tesla Roadstar, the company was burning through funds at an alarming rate. Musk was forced to cut the size of his team by 10% in 2007 to stave off financial disaster, and the following year *The Truth About Cars* website launched a "Tesla Death Watch", anticipating the end was nigh. *Valleywag*, the Silicon Valley gossip blog, had also earmarked Tesla its #1 tech company fail of 2007. Thankfully for Musk, they had both underestimated Musk's determination and the appeal of the Tesla product to investors.

Lesson 24: People will always try to rain on your parade. Keep your head down, keep working and ignore idle gossip. This is the only way to remain focus and not get bogged down by other people's negativity.

Elon said 'I will spend my last dollar on these companies. If we have to move into Justine's parents' basement, we'll do it.'

Antonio Gracias

Musk raised round after round of funding. He was confident, enthused constantly about Tesla and its potential, and investors believed what he had to say. He raised $45 million for the company in May 2007, $40 million in December 2008, and a further $50 million from Germany's Daimler AG (the makers of Mercedes-Benz) in May 2009. Musk had also contributed an estimated $70 million of his own money.

Now the company's fortunes began to turn for the better. Tesla delivered its first 147 cars by January 2009, showing that they were a credible prospect. Abu Dhabi's Aabar Investments bought 40% of Daimler AG's interest in Tesla and the company was advanced $465 million in loans from the United States Department of Energy part of the Advanced Technology Vehicles Manufacturing Loan Program. Mainstream car manufacturers Ford and Nissan also received funds from this programme, but Tesla was able to repay its loan well in advance of its competitors.

Lesson 25: Investment and growth are all about confidence. When one investor comes onboard and in doing so endorses your business, others will more than likely follow. The challenge is getting that first one to say "Yes"!

Tesla finally turned a profit for the first time in July 2009 on the back of sales of the Tesla Roadster.109 vehicles had shipped that month and as the company's fortunes now looked promising, Musk decided that the time was right for an initial public offering (IPO).

Tesla Motors launched its initial public offering on NASDAQ (the US-Canadian stock exchange) in June 2010. 13,300,000 shares were issued, each with a value of $17. IPO raised $226 million for the company, and it proved the catalyst for the company's epic growth: by the end of 2014 the share price had reached $240 per share and the total value of the company was nearly $29 billion. Tesla was the top performing company on the Nasdaq 100 index in 2013 and sold more than 33,000 cars worldwide in 2014.

Lesson 26: Right from the start you should know what your exit strategy for your company will be, and what the necessary conditions are for that exit. When the time is right, don't be afraid to let go. This is, after all, what you have been working for all along.

Although Tesla's long term goal is to produce cars for the mainstream consumer car market, in the meantime they are having fun creating some top end products that excite the automotive media. It is a shrewd business model because it creates aspiration, an appetite for Tesla's future products as and when they do become affordable for ordinary, middle class customers. The latest Tesla car the Model X SUV, was launched in September 2015 with a basic model costing around $80,000. If you want the top-of-the-range Signature Series, the prices rise to at least $132,000. The vehicle is exceptionally energy efficient, as you would expect from Tesla Motors, but there are also a number of other interesting features: the car continually scans the road with camera, radar and sonar systems so that it can automatically break before an accident and steer away from side collisions; the wing doors allow access in narrow spaces but also have sensors so that they won't crunch up into the roof of a garage; and the car can do 0 to 60 mph in 3.2 seconds. The Signature Series has a top speed of 275 mph (443 kmph).

Lesson 27: Creating aspiration creates demand for your brand. It is far easier to start at the top, selling and building a reputation for quality, than to begin at the bottom end of the market and to try to claw your way up.

Tesla's innovations are not just in the car market, however: Musk wants to bring affordable electrical energy into all walks of life. This is especially true regarding batteries. A Tesla batter is made up of thousands of lithium-ion 18650 commodity cells, typically used in laptops and other small consumer electrical devices. Made by Panasonic (itself an investor in Tesla), the cells are small, lightweight and cheap, costing around $200 per kWh, significantly less than any batter alternatives currently available on the market.

Lesson 28: Be aware of all the essential components in the product you sell. Their quality, reliability and cost will have a significant impact on your end product too.

Taking these batteries a step further, Tesla announced the Powerwall home and battery packs in April 2015. The standard version is a 7 kilowatt-hour wall-mounted unit, although industrial users can also opt for far larger batteries in units of 100 kWh. These will at first be made by Panasonic, then from 2016 onwards by Reno as this will enable Tesla to cut costs by around 30%. The move into household energy storage is hugely important because it means that for the first time consumers with solar panels on their houses can actually store the energy they produce in a cost effective manner. *Bloomberg* reported that Tesla consequently made $800 million of battery sales in their first week, smashing even Musk's expectations. Once it is operational, Musk's planned "Gigafactory" in Nevada will enable Tesla to more than double the world's total annual production of lithium-ion batteries. He is taking on the energy market in a spectacular manner.

Lesson 29: There is money to be made reworking your existing products in new and imaginative ways. Think outside the box for ways you can enter new markets.

Musk's interest in energy is not just in storage and use, but also in production. SolarCity, one of the USA's largest solar power companies, designs, finances, and installs solar power systems. Although it was founded in 2006 by Lyndon and Peter Rive, the idea for the company came from their cousin, Elon Musk, who is SolarCity's Chairman and provided its start-up capital.

SolarCity works in a number of complementary areas. It has a number of commercial solar installations in California, including on sites belonging to eBay, British Motors, Walmart and Intel; it offers energy efficiency evaluations and upgrades to home owners; there is a five-year plan to build more than $1 billion in solar photovoltaic projects (predominantly rooftop solar panels) for military housing estates in the US; it produced electric car charging points; and also installs snap together solar panels. SolarCity plans to build a major new manufacturing facility in Buffalo, New York in order to manufacture high-efficiency solar modules. When it is completed, this will be the largest such plant in the US and will enable SolarCity to compete aggressively against manufacturers in China.

Lesson 30: No market or business exists in isolation. Be constantly on the look out for ways to collaborate and build relationships that will stand you in good stead in the future.

Supporting SolarCity - which now has a market capitalisation in excess of $6 billion - is a good move for Musk as it sits well with his investment in Tesla. Not only can SolarCity produce the quality car chargers Tesla needs, but the household batteries produced by Tesla can also be used to store electricity produced by homes with SolarCity's photovoltaic cells. It is a win-win situation.

Musk's venture into public transportation, Hyperloop, is as yet just an idea on the drawing board, but if his track record is anything to go by, even the most far fetched idea might just come to fruition.

At its most basic, the Hyperloop is a theoretical high-speed transport system where pressurised capsules ride on a cushion of air through reduced pressure tubes, driven by linear induction motors and air compressors. Musk proposed the system to run parallel to Interstate 5 between Los Angeles and San Francisco in California, a journey of 354-mile (570 km). Musk believes that his system could cut the journey time to only 35 minutes, requiring an average speed of about 598 mph (962 km/h). Not only will this be significantly faster than any other available option, including air travel, but it would also substantially reduce congestion and traffic pollution on California's roads.

Lesson 31: Apply your expertise to real world problems if you really want to have a positive impact on the world in which you live.

Musk first proposed his idea for a "fifth mode of transport" in Santa Monica, California in 2011. He was addressing attendees at a web and tech event and spoke of his dream of a transport option that was immune to bad weather, could not crash, had an average speed twice that of a typical jet, required little power, and could store energy for 24-hour operations. Musk envisaged his Hyperloop as being a "cross between a Concorde and a railgun and an air hockey table".

The physical challenges that the Hyperloop project faces are the impact of air resistance and friction when anything moves at high speed. Maglev - the use of magnetically levitating trains in evacuated tubes - in theory at least eliminates these problems, but is an exceptionally expensive type of technology and it is difficult to maintain the necessary vacuum over any kind of distance.

To see if he could make it happen, Musk put together a team of engineers from Tesla and SpaceX. They worked on the conceptual foundation and modelling of Hyperloop and produced a white paper, inviting comment from the wider tech-minded community. Unusually, the design was open source: Musk wanted anyone to be able to understand it and to contribute ideas that might improve the design. He then announced his plan to build a prototype to test the concept in practice.

You want to be extra rigorous about making the best possible thing you can. Find everything that's wrong with it and fix it. Seek negative feedback, particularly from friends.

Elon Musk

Lesson 32: Commercial secrecy, though understandable, is an outdated model. You will make progress far faster if you can access the 'hive mind' of the wider community and harness their ideas.

Although initially it was reported that the Hyperloop test track would be in Texas, Musk then concluded it would be more convenient to situate it in California's Quay Valley, next door to SpaceX's Hawthorne facility. Here there will be a 1 mile (1.6 km) test track where they can trial pod designs submitted as entries in a Hyperloop design competition.

Musk came up with the Hyperloop concept, but to take the project to the next level he is happy for others to contribute and to do the running. He has allowed JumpStarter Inc. to create Hyperloop Transportation Technologies (HTT), a research company which is using a crowd funding and collaboration approach to develop the transportation system. More than 100 engineers, all of whom have taken stock options instead of upfront payment, are working together on designs. They expect to have completed their first feasibility study by the end of 2015, but admit that they are at least 10 years away from opening a commercially viable

Hyperloop. HTT hopes that its IPO will raise $100 million to fund the project's development. They already have permission to build a 5-mile (8.0 km) test track alongside Interstate 5, and have also proposed a Hyperloop route between Los Angeles and Las Vegas.

Lesson 33: You don't have to be possessive about your ideas. If you really want something to succeed, be prepared to let others have a go at it if you don't have the skills or resources available to you at the time.

Initial calculations suggest that Musk's own version of the Hyperloop would be technically and commercially viable. Musk has suggested a price tag of $6 billion, though critics do think this is optimistically low, and in the alpha design he outlines a scenario where the Hyperloop covers its capital costs within 20 years. A one-way passenger ticket would be a very affordable $20. The challenges are likely to be scaremongering - every critic is terrified of spiralling costs - and the difficulty of moving support (financial and political) away from the state's current mega-project, California High-Speed Rail. The existing project inevitably has many vested interests and so focusing on an alternative route (such as Los Angeles to Texas) that does not bring the two projects into head to head conflict might be the best route forward.

Lesson 34: Vested interests can block even the best ideas. Look ahead and find ways to circumvent them so that your projects don't get mired in the mud.

Awards and Recognition

Musk's recognition is international in scope and touches on multiple disciplines. He is lauded as an inventor and innovator by universities and learned society's, is the darling of the business world, and a popular and respected figure by journalists too. There is space here to discuss only a small selection of his awards.

Lesson 35: In today's multi disciplinary world, it is not enough to be an expert in just one area. A true renaissance man will earn the appreciation of his peers in every field.

In *Background and Education* we looked at Musk's university career, and though he abandoned his own doctorate at Stanford University after only two days, other institutions have moved to recognise his contributions to technology regardless. In the UK, Surrey University (one of the world's foremost centres for the development of satellite technology) has awarded Musk an honorary doctorate (DUniv) in Aerospace Engineering, and he also has an honorary doctorate of Engineering and Technology from Yale University. His third honorary doctorate, this time in design, comes from the ArtCenter College of Design in Pasadena, California.

Recognising his contributions in the field of space technology, Musk was asked to serve on the United States National Academy of Sciences Aeronautics and Space Engineering Board. He received the 2007/08 American Institute of Aeronautics and Astronautics George Low award for his design of the Falcon 1, and also National Space Society's Von Braun Trophy and the Fédération Aéronautique Internationale's Gold Space Medal, both for this same outstanding achievement. The Kitty Hawk Foundation have recognised Musk as a Living Legend of Aviation, and in 2011 he received the Heinlein Prize for Advances in Space Commercialization, worth $250,000.

Lesson 36: Academic awards can enhance your credibility in the commercial world too. The two worlds, though they sometimes can appear to be poles apart, are in fact compatible and have mutual benefits.

As a businessman, Musk's line up of accolades is no less impressive. *R&D Magazine*, *Inc Magazine* and *Fortune* have all named him as their entrepreneur of the year (in 2007, 2007 and 2014 respectively). *Esquire* magazine listed Musk as one of the 75 most influential people of the 21st century, and in 2011 he also appeared in *Forbes'* "America's 20 Most Powerful CEOs 40 And Under". If that weren't enough to confirm his superstar status, in January 2015 an episode of *The Simpsons* entitled "The Musk Who Fell to Earth" was broadcast, poking fun at some of his inventions. Musk made a guest appearance.

Lesson 37: Even when selling high ticket items like space crafts and electronic cars, there is no harm in appealing to the general public through popular culture.

Politics and Beliefs

Often it is easy to spot the political leanings of a major businessman, especially in the US, but that is not the case with Musk: he has described himself as "half-Democrat, half-Republican... I'm somewhere in the middle, socially liberal and fiscally conservative." He has contributed to election campaigns for both of the mainstream political parties in the US.

Lesson 38: Politics, and indeed one's own political position, is not black and white. You can, and should, shift your allegiance as required by your commercial needs.

The donations are linked to Musk's lobbying efforts: he understandably lobbies hard on issues of importance to his companies. A report from the Sunlight Foundation found that SpaceX alone has spent $4 million lobbying both sides of Congress, and Musk himself has made $725,000 in campaign donations. His own campaign to win political support is "systematic and sophisticated". It is also consistent. SpaceX has its own in-house lobbyists and also works with the Washington-based lobbying group Patton Boggs LLP and other similar groups.

Lesson 39: When lobbying and making donations, focus on the causes that make most business sense. Consider these efforts as part of your core business development costs, and take them seriously.

Although Musk's own companies have been the recipients of government subsidies in the past, Musk has subsequently spoken out against this. He believes that a carbon tax, levied on those companies that are not environmentally friendly, is a far better policy than costly subsidies. His view is controversial, however: collectively SpaceX, Tesla Motors and SolarCity have benefited from an estimated $4.9 billion in government subsidies, and in their early days even these companies may not have been successful without it.

Lesson 40: If the criticism of hypocrisy is levelled at you, have a good reason for your change of heart.

One thing that is in no doubt at all is Musk's patriotism. Despite being born in South Africa and becoming a US national only as an adult, Musk is unashamedly pro-American. He has described his host country as "[inarguably] the greatest country that has ever existed on Earth" and "the greatest force for good of any country that's ever been". Whether or not you agree with him, you have to admire his enthusiasm, and the approach has certainly ensured he's a favourite amongst US politicians and investors alike.

Lesson 41: Playing to the gallery will earn you plenty of Brownie points amongst the elite. Look after your supporters, and they will look after you.

The conservative elements in the US tend to ignore Musk's religious beliefs (or rather lack thereof).

He is a rationalist, basing his personal views on his understanding of the laws of physics. He thinks that it is unlikely that religion and science could coexist. He does believe, however, that there is a significant chance that there simple life on other planets, perhaps something akin to mould growing in a petri dish. Musk has "hope that there is other intelligent life in the known universe" and thinks that statistically it is "probably more likely than not".

What concerns Musk is not extraterrestrial life but the threat posed to humanity by artificial intelligence, which he has described as "the most serious threat to the survival of the human race". He is very concerned about the lack of regulatory oversight, either an a national or international level, and when addressing the the MIT AeroAstro Centennial Symposium, he went on to say "There have been movies about this, you know, like Terminator – there are some scary outcomes. And we should try to make sure the outcomes are good, not bad."

I wouldn't say I have a lack of fear. In fact, I'd like my fear emotion to be less because it's very distracting and fries my nervous system.

Elon Musk

Lesson 42: If there is something out there that worries you or that you fear, be honest about it. Don't hide in the dark and hope that it goes away. Instead, think about what you can do to overcome the threat and tackle it head on.

Personal Life

I remember thinking it was a lot of drama, and that if I was going to put up with it, we might as well be married. I told him he should just propose to me.

Justine Musk

Musk met his first wife, Justine, whilst they were both students at Queen's University in Ontario, Canada. She was an aspiring writer, and he wooed her with ice cream and bunches of roses. She travelled to Japan to teach, but returned to the US to join Musk in Silicon Valley, and the couple married in January 2000. The board of x.com (later PayPal) urged the bride and groom to sign a postnuptial agreement protecting his newly acquired wealth, and the sense of economic inequality within the relationship, combined with Musk's alpha male tendencies, caused notable strain.

Lesson 43: The characteristics that make you successful in business are not necessarily characteristics which will serve you well in other aspects of your life.

Nothing could have prepared the Musks for the trauma to come, however. Their first son, Nevada Alexander Musk, was born in 2002. The same week that Musk sold PayPal, catapulting his wealth to in excess of $100 million, the 10-week old baby was put down for a nap and stopped breathing. Although he was resuscitated by paramedics, Nevada had been deprived of oxygen for too long and was brain dead. Three days later his life support machines were turned off. The cause of death was sudden infant death syndrome (SIDS).

Lesson 44: No amount of money makes you immune from personal tragedy. What is important is how you respond when that tragedy strikes.

Musk bottled up his emotions, refusing to talk with his wife about their loss. At first Justine grieved openly, but Musk decried this behaviour as "emotionally manipulative" and so she was forced to hide her pain. In spite of being caught in a spiral of depression, she returned to the IVF clinic and gave birth first to twins and then to triplets, five small boys in all. Griffin and Xavier were born in 2004, and Damian, Saxon and Kai followed in 2006.

On the face of it, the Musks had a perfect family set-up and social life. They lived in a 6,000-square-foot house in the Bel Air Hills, partied with Bono, Paris Hilton and Leonardo DiCaprio, and travelled everywhere by private jet. What was missing, sadly, was intimacy and mutual respect. Musk was obsessed with his work and paid little attention to his wife. She had sacrificed her successful literary career to raise their children and support him, but he was dismissive. An intelligent, capable woman in her own right, Justine had been reduced to no more than a trophy wife, and she understandably resented that fact.

Lesson 45: A successful marriage depends on mutual respect and balance. If it is important to you, you need to work as hard at your relationship as you do at your career.

Faced with a collapsing marriage, and a wife who craved equality in their partnership, Musk agreed to begin marriage counselling. He lasted just three sessions, then impatiently issued Justine with an ultimatum: either we fix this marriage today or I will divorce you tomorrow. No relationship can be rebuilt in a day. Musk filed for divorce the next morning.

Their divorce, in spring 2008, was messy. Although by signing the post-nup Justine had in theory signed away all her rights as a married person, including to communal property, but there was some debate as to whether or not Musk had fully disclosed his finances at the time of signing, which was a marital fiduciary duty. Resolution was a matter for the courts.

Lesson 46: If you are going to mix marriage and money, make sure the paperwork is sorted out before you start. If you don't, only the lawyers will win.

I would like to allocate more time to dating, though. I need to find a girlfriend. That's why I need to carve out just a little more time. I think maybe even another five to 10 — how much time does a woman want a week? Maybe 10 hours? That's kind of the minimum? I don't know.

Elon Musk

Just six weeks after Musk filed for divorce, he announced his engagement to British actress Talulah Riley. Though the relationship between his ex-wife and new fiancee could have been acrimonious, Justine took the unusual step of reaching out to her replacement (who she has never met) in an email:

"I would rather live out the French-movie version of things, in which the two women become friends and various philosophies are pondered, than the American version, in which one is "good" and one is "bad" and there's a huge catfight sequence and someone gets thrown off a balcony."

Riley responded, "Let's do as the French do."

Lesson 47: In every walk of life, civility makes things far, far easier for everyone involved.

I remember him saying, 'Being with me was choosing the hard path.' I didn't quite understand at the time, but I do now. It's quite hard, quite the crazy ride.

Talulah Riley

A graduate of Cheltenham Ladies College, Riley probably first caught Musk's eye when she appeared as Mary Bennet in the 2005 film of *Pride and Prejudice*. She also had roles in *St. Trinian's*, *The Boat that Rocked*, and *Dr. Who*. The couple married in Dornoch Cathedral in 2010, and their marriage lasted two years. The *Telegraph* reported that Riley received a $4.2 million divorce settlement, but the couple were oddly reconciled, albeit temporarily, in 2014. The current status of their relationship is open to debate: legally Musk and Riley are still married, but the *Associated Press* announced another split on 31 December 2014, this time with an alimony payout of $16 million in cash and assets.

Lesson 48: The prying and speculating of the press puts every high profile relationship under pressure. Be clear about what you are and are not prepared to share with the media and the public, and defend your right to privacy to that those around you are protected.

In spite of these payouts to his ex-wives, Musk still has ample fortune to spend. He distributes some of this philanthropically through the Musk Foundation. Reflecting his commercial interests, the Musk Foundation provides solar powered energy systems to communities which have been hit by natural disasters. Recent donations have included a 25 kW solar power system for the South Bay Community Alliance's (SBCA) hurricane response centre in Alabama, and a $250,000 contribution towards a solar power project in a tsunami-affected area of Japan. Philanthropy and charity are not the same thing, and Musk understands this implicitly. It is perfectly acceptable to use the former to raise your profile and awareness of your products and services. Doing good for others can do you and your business good too.

In addition to this, Musk has made donations to individual projects which interest him. He donated $1 million towards the construction of the Tesla Science Center at Tesla's former Wardenclyffe Laboratory on Long Island, New York, as well as pledging to build a Tesla Supercharger in the museum's car park, and he gave $10 million to the Future of Life Institute to fund their global research programme. The purpose of this was to ensure artificial intelligence (something which concerns Musk greatly, see *Politics and Beliefs*) remains a net benefit to humanity.

Lesson 49: Support only the things which really interest you. If you make money, every cat and dog home will come begging, but you don't have to fund them all. Use your money wisely.

The board of the X Prize Foundation, which designs competitions intended to encourage technological development that could benefit mankind, reads like a who's who of the tech and business worlds, so it should come as no surprise that Musk sits on the boar alongside Larry Page, Arianna Huffington, Ratan Tata and others. Musk's interest in the non-profit organisation was likely piqued by the Ansari XPRIZE, which is a $10 million prize for the first privately financed team that could build and fly a three-passenger vehicle 100 km into space twice within two weeks. This particular prize was won by Mojave Aerospace Ventures, whose spacecraft SpaceShipOne successfully completed the challenge in 2004. Its successor award is the Google Lunar XPRIZE, launched in 2007, which will give $20 million to the first team to land a rover on the moon. The rover must travel more than 500m and transmit back high definition images and video. Bonus prizes of $5 million each are available for teams whose rover can travel long distances (considered to be more than 5km) or can survive the lunar night.

Lesson 50: As an entrepreneur, you have a responsibility to inspire the next generation of innovators. Doing so may well be the greatest legacy you leave.

Conclusion

I think it is possible for ordinary people to choose to be extraordinary.

Elon Musk

It would be hard, and probably unfair, to argue that Elon Musk is not a genius. Though his academic credentials are not remarkable - he did abandon his PhD incomplete after all - his breadth and depth of understanding of science and technology, combined with his willingness to keep on learning new things, means that he is uniquely well placed to try and solve some of the many challenges faced today in our world. Unlike an elected politician, Musk is not answerable to an electorate. He doesn't have to make populist choices, and he can take on projects where the results will not be seen until quite some time along the line. He is also not like other businessmen. His companies do have shareholders, of course, but he is also prepared to put his own money into a project, to test it out and get things up and running to the point when the idea is proven and other investors want to jump on his band wagon. He sees his role in life not just being about making money, though he does have a competitive, acquisitive side too, but also about addressing the major issues that humanity faces, challenges that seem to huge and insurmountable at the start that others are afraid to even try.

I came to the conclusion that we should aspire to increase the scope and scale of human consciousness in order to better understand what questions to ask. Really, the only thing that makes sense is to strive for greater collective enlightenment.

Elon Musk

Perhaps Musk's greatest and most admirable asset is that he can look at the big picture and take the long view. He is not in a rush, and he does not have to prove himself to others. His achievement to date, in business and in innovation, already put him on a level far beyond what most other entrepreneurs and/or inventors can ever hope to achieve, so what Musk does now is entirely up to him. If a challenge interests him, and if an idea inspires him, he can pursue it and see where it leads. This gives Musk a great deal of freedom to try things out, and the freedom to think and to dream is something that all of his disciples can emulate. We may be restrained by physical and financial barriers, but that does not mean that we can't open our minds and look at the challenges we face in new and imaginative ways. When our thoughts are unencumbered, we will come up with the best solutions.

[Physics is] a good framework for thinking. ... Boil things down to their fundamental truths and reason up from there.

Elon Musk

Musk's life and work so far also teaches us that you don't have to be a specialist in one narrow field: a true renaissance man like Leonardo Da Vinci, Musk is able to think creatively, and to excel, in multiple disciplines. Yes, he has undoubtedly mastered the basics of mathematics and physics, engineering and computer programming, not to mention public speaking, leadership and self promotion, but he is not (yet) a Nobel prize winning scientist, and his oratory skills fall short of those of, for example, Winston Churchill or Adolf Hitler. What Musk does have is a breadth of interest and knowledge, enough to understand the complexities of arguments and the nuances of details presented to him. He is perpetually curious, even to the point of obsession, wanting to know more and more. He has learned to surround himself with the greatest thinkers and doers in each industry he wants to work in. He inspires and leads them, but depends very much on their collective input and expertise to make his projects happen. Musk's mastery of the dual arts of leadership and delegation is what enables him to rise above his competitors, to see further, and to achieve far more.

It would be perfectly possible to replicate Musk's educational and professional career moves step by step without achieving the same outcome. He is, like any successful entrepreneur, the beneficiary of a particular, fortunate set of circumstances. Had he made the same decisions, the same bids, at a different time in his career, the outcomes would likely have been very different: we have already seen how close SpaceX and Tesla Motors came to falling flat on their faces. The final lesson in this book which we should learn from Musk, then, is that what determines success is not your qualifications, where you were born, or how much money you have. Instead, it is how you choose to see the world, your openness to ideas, and how you respond to opportunities and challenges when you are faced with them. No one in this world, not even Elon Musk, goes through life with a completely easy ride. For all of us there are forks in the road, and vital decisions to be made. We must approach these times with confidence and conviction if we are to achieve our goals.

Thank you for purchasing my book! I know you could have picked from dozens of books about Elon Musk, but you took a chance with mine and I appreciate it.

Made in the USA
San Bernardino, CA
22 July 2018